Ladies, What Kind Of Man Are You Going To Marry?

Ladies, What Kind Of Man Are You Going To Marry?

A Guide To Help Single Women Align With Their God-Ordained Husbands

Stephanie Ross

Cover Design: Stephanie Ross

Photo: Bloom Photography

Editor: Patricia Ogilvie of ProriskEnterprises.com

For more information, please email the author at stephaniero.2012@yahoo.com

Table of Contents

Introduction

Single Ladies, it is mandatory that you read this book, *Ladies, What Kind of Man Are You Going to Marry?*

Ladies, the institution of marriage is suffering. The divorce rate is high. Even Christians are finding themselves divorcing. Many marriages are unhappy, void of God, and seem to have no real purpose. They have become unhealthy and unfulfilling. This book is a guide to help single women align with their God ordained husbands. It will help you to uncover any warning signs or clues that can help prevent you from marrying the wrong man and bring you into alignment with who God has for you.

1

The Definition of Marriage

Chapter 1

The Definition of Marriage

T o understand marriage better, we need to turn to the Word of God. There is no better guide to live by and to find the understanding of marriage. The Word of God is filled with Bible verses on love and guidance for couples' marriages. People who truly desire a godly marriage will seek God's Word for wisdom and understanding concerning marriage. It's unfortunate that so many couples miss the mark before they say, "I Do." They lack the godly wisdom needed to sustain a marriage, which can only be found in the word of God. They get married without truly understanding the biblical meaning of what marriage really is. They say "I Do" but never apply the Word of God to their marriages.

They choose to ignore Jesus' teaching in Matthew 7:24-27 on Building on a Rock that says, "Therefore whoever hears these sayings of Mine, and does them, I will liken him to a wise man who built his house on a rock: and the rain descended, the floods came, and it did not fall, for it was founded on the rock. But everyone who hears these sayings of Mine, and does not do them, will be like a foolish man who built his house on the sand: and the rain came, beat on that house; and it fell. And great was its fall." Some couples choose to build their marriages on a foundation of sand and believe that should a storm come, their marriages will be able to withstand it.

Couples' marriages should be built on a rock, which is Jesus Christ. If a crisis should show up in their marriages because it is a marriage that is built on a solid foundation, it will be able to withstand the storm. Even when the rain descends and the floods come, their marriage will not fall.

The Bible defines marriage as a covenant. When God designed marriage, He said that it was good. The first covenanted marriage can be found in Genesis 2:21-24 between Adam and Eve. "And the LORD God caused a deep sleep to fall on Adam, and he slept; and He took one of his ribs and closed up the flesh in its place. Then the rib which the LORD had taken from man He made into a woman, and He brought her to the man. And Adam said, 'This is now bone of my bones and flesh of my flesh; She shall be called Woman, because she was taken out of Man.' Therefore, a man shall leave his father and mother and be joined to his wife, and they shall become one flesh." The Bible says that when Adam saw Eve, he said, "This is now bone of my bones and flesh of my flesh; she shall be called Woman, because she was taken out of Man." Adam goes on to say, "Therefore, a man shall leave his father and mother and be joined to his wife, and they shall become one flesh." You see, once Adam and Eve were joined together, into a single entity, they became one flesh. Adam and Eve entered into a covenanted marriage that was divinely orchestrated by God. Adam wrote his vows, and God officiated the marriage.

When couples get married, they enter into a holy covenant with God. It is an act that is committed before God and man. The word covenant is defined as an agreement. Before couples get married, both parties need to understand the full extent of their committee. Often, all too many times, couples treat their marriages as some kind of job rather than a holy covenant. They fill out the job application (the Marriage license). They accept the job (consent to the Marriage). They work at the job for several years (the Marriage). Then they become bored with the job (the Marriage), and they want to quit (the Marriage). They file for a divorce (a certificate of divorce). And they go their separate ways. Not one time realizing that they have broken a holy covenant with God. But why make the mistake in the first place? Why marry someone but then end up divorcing them? When God ordains a marriage, there will be no room for error, and no man can separate it.

The perfect marriage is modeled between Christ and his Bride, which is the church. It represents our spiritual relationship with God. Bible scriptures make it very clear that marriage is a holy and divinely established covenant. But many couples ignore this teaching and instead mistreat and abuse marriage. Some couples treat marriage as though it's just some kind of arrangement that can be forfeited if it doesn't work out. Ladies, marry a man that will work at treating your marriage as a spiritual relationship with God, as a holy, and divinely established covenant, and not just as an arrangement that he can separate from if things are not working out.

Couples should seek God to be a part of their marriages. We have already established that a couple's marriage should be built on the foundation of Jesus Christ. so that, should a storm come, the marriage will be able to withstand it. We have also established that couples should seek the word of God as a guide to understand marriage better. But often, couples neglect this teaching. They jump into the marriage and fail to apply the Bible's principles concerning marriage.

Most couples enter their marriages believing that they are two different individuals who have entered a committed relationship. Often, couples marry but still live separate lives, pursuing two distinct purposes and visions. But marriage should be looked at as a partnership where couples work together in unity and with one accord. The Bible says that God now sees them as "One Flesh." Genesis 2:24 says, "For this reason a man shall leave his father and mother and be joined to his wife; and they shall become one flesh." The Bible says that after you are married, you now have become one flesh. Not literally one piece of flesh, but spiritually speaking, you are now one person, one purpose, and one vision. Eve came to the Garden to help Adam with his assignment. Adam and Eve worked together, not separately; they had one purpose and the same vision. But often, couples get married then decide to live two different lives. They are driven in two different directions, apart from each other and apart from God. There becomes a pull on the marriage because they are trying to operate outside of one another. She's doing one thing, and he's doing something else. She's pursuing her purpose, and he's pursuing his, never coming together in one accord. Remember, it was only when Eve tried to pull apart from Adam that she messed up. How can one flesh operate as two? So many times, couples miss or just choose to neglect this teaching.

Adam and Eve worked together as one unit with one another. They had one assignment and a clear vision of what that assignment was before entering into the marriage. God gave them the assignment, and they implemented it. Adam's assignment was to work and take care of the Garden of Eden, and Eve's was to help her husband with the task that God had given him.

Ladies, enter into a marriage with a man that already has a clear vision of what his assignment from God is. And with a man who has a clear vision of what the definition of marriage really is. God will never send you to a man that is confused or unclear of these things. You see, Adam already had a clear vision of what his godly assignment was long before Eve arrived. And he was clear of the definition of marriage before Eve was brought to him. Adam completely comprehended what marriage really was; that's why when he saw Eve, he could declare, "She is bone of my bones and flesh of my flesh." God will never send you to a man that is not ready to be a husband.

The definition of marriage should be known by the man that you are going to marry. Ladies, be cautious of marrying a man who is ill-prepared in this area. Remember, you have been sent to help your husband with the assignment that God has already given to him. But how can you help him with this assignment if he has no revelation of what the assignment is? Or how can the man lead you if he has no clue of where he's going? And how can he guide you if he doesn't know who to follow? Eve was able to help Adam with the assignment that God had given to Adam. You see, Adam was able to lead Eve because he was following God.

Couples need to follow God's instruction concerning marriage, and it will remain in love. If couple's marriages are not founded on God's Principles, it will be confusion, a lack of understanding and uncertainty. And we know that with God, there is no room for error therefore, there will be nothing concerning the marriage that will be incorrect or wrong. God's Word gives a clear definition of what marriage is and if couples would follow these instructions, their marriages will be blessed. Just as God blessed Adam and Eve's marriage, He will bless yours as well.

Marriage is by God's design and for His pleasure and to whomever He pleases. God's design for marriage is that the covenant made between the man and woman be unbreakable and unshakable. Marriages are not for the couples, but for God. He uses them for His will and for His glory. Marriage should be for couples who have a clear vision of their assignments from God, and are operating in those assignments, implementing what God has given them. Marriage should be for couples who can work together to help cultivate God's kingdom. Marriage should be for couples who will use their marriages only for the glory of God. And marriage should be for couples who can love each other like Christ loves His church.

The definition of marriage is 1 Corinthians 13:13 says, "And now these three remain: faith, hope, and love. But the greatest of these is love." Notice what is listed as the greatest of these three that remain, "LOVE." These three things are needed for a marriage to be successful. But most of all, the greatest thing that is needed in a marriage is "LOVE." Couples that desire to be married should truly understand this verse. A marriage needs faith, it needs hope, but most of all, a marriage needs love.

In order that faith, hope and love to remain in a marriage, it will need Jesus. He is the only One who can sustain a marriage in these three things. Jesus gave all believers the promise of the Holy Spirt. And it is because of Him that a marriage will have the ability to remain in faith, continue in hope, and in love, just as Jesus loves.

The definition of marriage is found in 1 Corinthians 13:4-7, "Love is patient, love is kind. It does not envy, it does not boast, it is not proud. It does not dishonor others, it is not self-seeking, it is not easily angered, it keeps no record of wrongs. Love does not delight in evil but rejoices with the truth. It always protects, always trust, always hopes, always perseveres." A couples' marriage should be bound to this scripture. They should tie them as symbols around their wrist, bind them on their foreheads, write them on the doorframes of their houses and fix them in their hearts and minds. This scripture should flow from the abundance of their hearts.

The definition of marriage is Colossians 3:14 says, "And over all these virtues put on love, which binds them all together in perfect unity." The word Love is expressed repeatedly in these Bible verses. Couples need to understand that for a marriage to have a perfect unity, it must have love. Love is the thing that will sustain a couple's marriage when they're just not getting along. Love is the thing that will bring the two of them back together after a disagreement. Love is the thing that will keep the two of them together in perfect unity when they have had enough and contemplating divorce. Love is the thing that helps them stay together in sickness and in health. Love is the thing that when they fight, they can make up. And love is the thing that if they should contemplate getting into bed with someone else, they won't.

The definition of marriage in 1 Peter 4:8 says, "Above all, love each other deeply, because love covers over a multitude of sins." Couples need to apply this scripture to their marriage. They should understand that in their imperfect marriage, love will cover it.

2

Adam and Eve, The First God Ordained Marriage

Chapter 2

Adam and Eve, The First God Ordained Marriage

hy did God create marriage, what is the meaning of marriage, what is the purpose of marriage, and why should couples get married? There are so many questions concerning marriage. People seek understanding about marriage from their friends, their family, and maybe even a marriage counselor. But to better understand marriage, you need to turn to the Word of God. There is no better guide to live by and find an understanding of marriage than in God's Word. Let's start with the couple Adam and Eve so that we can get a clearer picture of the Bible's first God ordained marriage. Their love story can be found in the Book of Genesis.

The Bible says in Genesis 2:18-24, "Then the LORD God said, 'It is not good that the man should be alone; I will make him a helper fit for him.' Now out of the ground, the LORD God had formed every beast of the field and every bird of the heavens and brought them to the man to see what he would call them. And whatever the man called every living creature, that was its name. The man gave names to all livestock and to the birds of the heavens and to every beast of the field. But for Adam there was not found a helper fit for him. So, the LORD God caused a deep sleep to fall upon the man, and while he slept, took one of his ribs and closed its place with flesh. And the rib that the LORD God had taken from the man he made into a woman and brought her to the man. Then the man said, this is bone of my bones and flesh of my flesh; she shall be called Woman, because she was taken out of Man. Therefore, a man shall leave his father and mother and hold fast to his wife, and they shall become one flesh." God was the matchmaker for Adam and Eve. Adam and Eves' marriage was a covenant that was designed by God, for God. It was for His purpose and His Glory.

Notice that Genesis 2:18 starts out by saying, then the LORD God said, "It is not good that the man should be alone; I will make him a helper fit for him." God said that it was not good that Adam should be alone. God saw that Adam needed a companion, someone compatible with him. God didn't just bring Adam any kind of woman, but He brought Adam a helper that was fit for him. Adam and Eve were well matched, like-minded, of the same mind and from the same God. Eve was a woman that was handmade by the Hand of God. Eve was like Adam. She came to help him. To make life easier for Adam. God had given Adam an assignment where he was to tend and keep the garden of Eden. I believe that for Adam to complete God's assignment fully, he would need Eve's help. Eve was brought to Adam to help fulfill a need of loneliness, to turn something that was not good into something good, and to help him with his God-given assignment.

Adam had been called by God to tend and keep it in the garden of Eden. God was preparing Adam for marriage. God gave Adam a job, an assignment, and a purpose before he gave him a wife. God didn't make the woman first, but the animals. Adam had to first grow and be cultivated in the presence of God. Notice that the one thing that Adam and the Eve had in common was that they both knew God and He knew them. Adam and Eve worked together to fulfill their God-given purposes.

It's interesting that Adam was able to identify Eve as his wife. Earlier, God had brought Adam all the animals to name. Adam called the lion a lion and the sheep he called a sheep. But when God brought the Women to Adam, he called her wife. What was it about

16

this creation that Adam could recognize that it was different from what God had brought him earlier?

You see, Adam had become wise in the presence of God. Adam realized that Eve was godsent because God brought her to him. God personally brought the Woman to Adam. God was the matchmaker. He took one rib from the Adam and made one woman, which would have me to believe the one woman was all Adam needed. When God brought the Woman to Adam, he recognized the women as his wife. He knew that she was different from what God had brought him earlier. Adam had an instance connection with the Woman as soon as she arrived. Eve was a part of Adam by way of his rib. Adam had always been in the presence of God. So, when the Woman came, he could recognize her as his wife. Adam knew that because this woman had come from his very own rib, that it was a divine connection from God. I believe that Adam could recognize Eve as his wife because he knew God as his creator. And because Adam knew God as his creator, he could recognize Eve as his wife.

You see, Eve didn't have to prove to Adam who she was, because Adam already understood Eve's purpose when she arrived. All she had to do was stand right where God had positioned her, and it was up to Adam to do the rest. Eve didn't have to pressure Adam into marrying her. God showed Adam, Eve, and Adam identified who Eve was right away; he called her his "Wife." Adam didn't have to guess or wonder where this woman had come from; he understood that Eve had come from God Himself. He didn't waste time trying to figure out if she was the right fit for him. Adam understood that Eve was the person that God had aligned him to be with.

Adam recognized immediately that Eve was his wife. Adam recognized Eve as his wife because he first knew God as his creator. He didn't need months or years to decide that he wanted

Eve to be his wife. Adam didn't need to make up his mind, his mind was already made up. Adam was a godly man who stood on godly principles. He not only walked with God, but he also obeyed Him. In Genesis 2:23, when Adam said that "This is now bone of my bone and flesh of my flesh; She shall be called Woman, because she was taken out of Man." I believe that when Adam declared these words, that he was speaking directly to God.

God brought Eve to Adam to be his wife because she was like Adam. She was comparable to him. Which means Eve was like him. She had qualities in common with Adam.

Ladies, when God brings you to the man, will he be able to recognize that you are different from anything that he has ever he had before? And just like Adam, will he see you and call you, his wife? Will he declare the same thing that Adam declared in Genesis 2:18, that you are now bone of his bones and flesh of his flesh? Remember, God brought Eve to Adam, but it was up to Adam to recognize Eve as his wife. Will the man be so close to God, that when he sees you, he will know that you were sent from God, for him? Will he be so close to God, that when God reviles you to him that he will know that you are the very rib that has come from his side. Will he be so close to God that he will let it be known in the presence of God and man, by a vow, that you are his wife, and this is what God has joined together?

I believe that just like God created Eve for Adam, He has also created you for your godly ordained husband. And by the hand of God, you will be assigned to him at the appointed time. And just like God saw that it was not good that the man Adam should be alone, God sees the same for your husband. And just like God took a rib from Adam and made Eve, God has taken a rib from your God ordained husband and made you. And just like God brought Eve to Adam, He's going to bring you to your husband. God knows when the man that you are going to marry is ready to be your husband. And when he's ready to be a husband, God will send you to be his wife.

Ladies, stay faithful to God, and He will bring you into alignment with your husbands. God will bring you to the man at the appointed time, who will need her help to fulfill his assignment. God was the One who looked at Adam and thought that it was not good that he should be alone. So, He chose to make Adam a helper that would be fit for him. And just like God looked at Adam and saw the need for him to have a wife, He also has looked at the man that you are going to marry and examined him and understands that his loneness is not good for him. So, at the appointed time, God will align you with him to help fulfill his need for loneliness.

3

Bible Marriages, With A God Divined Purpose

Chapter 3

Bible Marriages, With A God Divined Purpose

T he word purpose is defined as the reason for which something is done, created, or for which something exists. The Bible gives some perfect examples of couples who were created then joined together for God's divine purpose. Their marriages were from God, for His glory, and to help accomplish His perfect will. These marriages were all divine setups by God. Whenever God joins couples together in a holy covenant, He will always have a plan for their marriages. Before God joined these couples together, He already had an end goal in mind. Their covenanted marriages were used by God so that through them, Jesus Christ would be born.

Whenever God is the matchmaker, it is only because He is going to use a couple's marriage as part of His perfect and divine will that through their marriages, He will get the glory. When God chooses a couple's marriage, then He can use it for His good, accomplishing some excellent things. When a couples' marriage is by God's design, great things will happen, bringing God's plan into existence.

Listed below are some perfect examples of marriages that God used for His divine will. God joined these couples together and then used their marriages for His good and His glory. These couples' marriages were divine setups by God. Their marriages were arranged and established by God to help bring about His perfect will. God always has a reason for what He does. From these

God aligned marriages came prophets, kings, priests, and Jesus Christ.

Let's open the book to some of these amazing Bible marriages and turn the pages to see just how God used these couples' marriages to help bring about His perfect will. These Bible marriages were by God's design. These couples were chosen by God for His purpose. They were used as vessels to bring about God's plan. Their marriages were spiritual, established, and ordered by God.

Abraham and Sarah

Abraham and Sarah were a couple whose marriage was used by God to help bring about His Perfect will. Abraham and Sarah's marriage was by God's design, for His purpose and His glory.

Their love story can be found in Genesis, Chapter 17. Abraham was married to Sarah. Sarah was barren and not able to have any children. But then God promised Abraham that He would be the father of many nations, and that Sarah would conceive and bear a son named Isaac. That this child would be the fulfillment of God's promise to Abraham and his descendants after him. God told Abraham that He would then bless Sarah, and that she would be the mother of many nations; kings of peoples would come from her. Then Abraham fell on his face and laughed, and said in his heart, "Shall a child be born to a man who is one hundred years old? And shall Sarah, who is ninety years old, bear a child?" But God assured Abraham that Sarah would indeed bear a son, and that they shall call his name Isaac. God promised that He would establish an everlasting covenant, with Abraham and his descendants.

Through Abraham and Sarah's marriage came Isaac, who God would use to help establish an everlasting covenant. Abraham and Sarah's marriage had a promise from God. He used their marriage to help bring about His perfect and divine will. Their marriage was used as part of His design and for His glory.

Zechariah and Elizabeth

Zechariah and Elizabeth's marriage was used as part of God's divine purpose. Their marriage was by God's design and for His glory. Their love story can be found in Luke Chapter 1. The Bible says that Zechariah and Elizabeth were both righteous, and that they were walking in all the commandments and ordinances of the Lord blameless. But they had no child, because Elizabeth was baren, and that they both were well advanced in years.

The Bible says that one day while Zachariah was in the temple burning incense, an Angel of the LORD appeared to him. The angel said to Zachariah that his prayers had been heard and that his wife Elizabeth would bear a son, and that they were to name him John. The angel told Zachariah that they would have great gladness and that many would rejoice at the child's birth. That the child would be great in the sight of the LORD, that the child was specially chosen by the LORD, and that he would turn many of the children of Israel to the LORD their God.

Elizabeth and Zachariah's child grew older and was known to us all as John the Baptist. John preached the message of repentance to the people to prepare their hearts for faith in Jesus Christ. God used Zachariah and Elizabeth's marriage as part of His perfect will. Their marriage was by God's design and for His purpose. Zachariah and Elizabeth's marriage was used by God to bring forth the prophet John the Baptist, who was used as a forerunner of the promised Messiah. The thing that was birthed through Zachariah's and Elizabeth's marriage was used as part of God's perfect will. Zachariah and Elizabeth' child was used to help save God's lost people, and to help lead them to salvation in faith in Jesus Christ.

Ladies, God used Zachariah and Elizabeth's marriage to help establish His perfect divine will. He impregnated their marriage for His purpose and for His glory. The things that come from Zachariah's and Elizabeth's marriage was chosen by God.

4

A Man Like Adam

Chapter 4

A Man Like Adam

In the Book of Genesis Chapter 7, we find Adam. Adam was the very first man ever to exist. God created Adam and placed him in the Garden of Eden to tend to and keep it. He was in the very essence of paradise. God allowed Adam to name every animal that He created. I would say that Adam had a pretty good life. Adam was placed in this garden by God just for him. He was in this Garden of Eden, and in the very presence of God. God had a very special relationship with Adam. You see, God had previously spoken everything into existence. But with Adam, something special happened. Genesis Chapter 2 talks about how God got down on the ground in the dirt and formed Adam out of clay. God breathed His breath into Adam's nostrils, and he became a living soul. God's very breath had been breathed into the Adam's nostrils. God had gotten very up close and personal with Adam.

Adam was alone in the Garden working, tending, and keeping the garden of Eden. Then God looked at Adam and saw that he needed a companion. It was probably a little lonely in the huge garden. He had no companion to talk to. Yes, there were lots of animals that he could talk to. But God saw that the animals were just not a good fit. So, God brought Adam a wife by the name of Eve. What I love about Adam, is that he was carrying out the assignment that God had purposed for his life. God had given Adam a job, and that was to tend and keep the garden of Eden. I also like that Adam had a personal relationship with God. He had an intimate closeness with his creator. Adam was enjoying God and God was enjoying him. It was God and Adam, Adam, and God. No distractions, nothing to draw his attention away from God. He had to grow and mature in the things of God. Adam needed to be implementing his assignment, tending to what God had given him to do. But most of all, he had to spend time alone with God.

What made Adam ready for marriage? Well, Adam was in the very presence of God. He had a personal relationship with Him. God knew Adam and Adam knew God. Adam was also being obedient to the assignment that God had given him. He was working, tending, and keeping the garden of Eden. I believe that because of Adam's intimate and personal relationship with God, that God blessed Adam with a wife.

God brought Eve to Adam, when He knew that Adam was ready, in a suitable state, and fully prepared to be a husband.

Adam was in a position of readiness. He was ready to be a husband, and he was ready to receive his wife. God wanted to bless Adam. God loved Adam so much that He didn't want to see him alone. He knew what His plans were for Adam. Adam's declaration later would be Proverbs 18:22 that says, "He who finds a wife finds a good thing and obtains favor from the LORD." Adam obtained favor from the LORD, when God blessed him with a wife. God showed Adam kindness beyond what was due or usual. God understood that Adam needed Eve to fully complete his life. Adam didn't realize that he was lonely, until God brought Eve to his attention.

Remember, the Bible calls Eve a helpmate. God saw that it was not good that Adam should be alone, so He formed Eve from Adam's very own rib and brought her to him. Genesis Chapter 2 says that the LORD God caused a deep sleep to fall upon the man, and while he slept took one of his ribs and closed its place with flesh. And the rib that the LORD God had taken from the man He made into a woman and brought her to the man.

It was like God had brought back to Adam literally a piece of himself. Eve was taken from Adam and then perfectly designed by God, and then, given back to Adam. God didn't need Adam's input. So, He caused a deep sleep to fall upon Adam. God didn't need Adam to tell him what kind of woman he wanted; God infinitely knew that it wasn't what Adam wanted, but what Adam needed. God didn't even consult Adam on the matter. I believe that Adam's input would have just been a distraction in what God was trying to do for him. It's interesting how God didn't just speak Eve into existence, but that He took from the Adam his very own rib and made the Eve.

In the Bible, Genesis 2:18 God said, "That it is not good that the man should be alone; I will make him a helper suitable for him." Eve was Adam's helper. This is the only part of God's creation that He declared was not good. In earlier chapters, when God created anything, He said that it was good. But with Adam, God looked at the man in his singleness, and saw that it was not good. God intervened and did something to change the man's loneliness. God had the perfect solution to the thing that He said was not good, a wife.

Adam had such a deep and intimate relationship with God, that God took Adam's very own rib from his side and in perfection, He made Eve. The dictionary defines a rib as, a long-raised piece of stronger or thicker material across a surface or through a structure, and typically serving to support or strengthen it. Notice the words "support and strengthen." Wow, God could have created Eve the same way that He created Adam, from the dust of the ground. But He chose to subtract from Adam to add him a wife. God took from Adam and then gave him Eve. God gave Adam something good, He gave Adam a wife, someone who was comparable to him. Eve was like Adam because she came from him. Adam declared in

Genesis 2:23, "This is bone of my bones and flesh of my flesh; She shall be called Woman Because she was taken out of Man."

God knew that Adam needed companionship. God knew the Adam was incomplete. But when God made Eve and brought her to Adam, the man became complete. Eve put an end to Adam's loneliness. After Eve's arrival, there was nothing else that needed to be added or changed in Adams's life. Adam had a relationship with God before Eve came. Adam was able to love Eve the way that God loved him. Adam was able to care for Eve the same way that God cared for him. Adam could now provide for Eve the way God had provided for him. Adam spoke in Proverbs 18:22 that says, "He who finds a wife finds a good thing and obtains favor from the LORD." Adam saw Eve as a blessing, an obtained favor from God?

Ladies, will the man that you marry, like Adam, have such a deep and intimate relationship with God, that God will cause him to fall asleep, take his rib from his side and make you? Will he, like Adam, recognize you as his wife, and declare what Adam declared in Genesis 2:23, "This is bone of my bones and flesh of my flesh; She shall be called Woman Because she was taken out of Man?" Will he see you like Adam saw Eve as a blessing, an obtained favor from God, and declare Proverbs 18:22 that says, "He who finds a wife finds a good thing and obtains favor from the LORD."

Will he recognize that because he has found you, that he has found a good thing, and that God has shown him an act of kindness beyond what is due or usual. Will he recognize that he has been singled out by God to receive a divine reward? Adam put himself in the right position to receive his blessing, a wife. And just like when Adam was in the right position to receive Eve, will the man that you marry be in the right position to receive you?

5

A Man Like Abraham

Chapter 5

A Man Like Abraham

W hen I think about Abraham, two things come to mind: Faith and obedience. Abraham was tested over-and-over again by God, yet he never wavered in his faith. When God sent Abraham the test, he passed every time. The Bible says in James 2:23, And the scripture was fulfilled that says, "Abraham believed God, and it was counted to him as righteousness, and he was called God's friend."

Abraham was tested by God. And he was called by God. Abraham's first test came in Genesis 12:1:3, the LORD had said to Abraham, "Go from your country and your kindred and your father's house to the land that I will show you. And I will make you a great nation, and I will bless you and make your name great, so that you will be a blessing. I will bless those who bless you, and him who dishonors you I will curse, and in you the families of the earth shall be blessed."

Abraham was not a young man when God told him to pack up and leave. He was seventy-five years old. He was probably at a comfortable place in his life. Abraham was with all his family and friends. A place where he had been all his life. This was a place where Abraham was familiar with. But when God told Abraham to pack up and leave, in his obedience and by faith he listened to God. Abraham, along with his wife Sarah, at God's word, packed up all his possessions and left his home and traveled to the land of Canaan. God called Abraham out of his home, a place that he had been all his life, to go to a strange land that he had never been.

31

Abraham had to trust God. All Abraham had was God's Word.

God promised Abraham three things: The first promise was that he would give Abraham his own land. The second promise was that he would make Abraham a great nation. And the third promise was of a blessing.

Abraham believed God for these three promises. He didn't question God. He was obedient to God, and in his obedience, God was able to bless Abraham. Abraham had great faith. He modeled walking by faith and not by sight. Abraham's faith pleased God. It was by faith that Abraham could leave everything that he knew and go to a land that he did not know. Hebrews 11:8 says, "By faith Abraham obeyed when he was called to go out to a place that he was to receive as an inheritance." And he went out, not knowing where he was going. Abraham lived a life of obedience through his faith in God.

Faith is needed in a couple's marriage. It is something that is needed should God send a test. Faith is something that should be in place, should the enemy try to attack a couple's marriage. With faith, a couple's marriage will be able to sustain a test, because faith is the thing needed to counterattack in response to one made by the enemy. Without faith in a couple's marriage, when a test comes, the marriage might not pass the test and fail. Faith is what Abraham needed in his marriage when God told him to pack up and go, he did by faith. Without faith, Abraham might have doubted God and forfeited the blessing that God had for him. Abraham had to move by faith and not by sight. He had to trust God at His word. And Sarah had to trust her husband at the word that God had given to him. A couple's marriage needs a foundation of faith.

When couple's marriages are faced with challenging or hard decisions, it will be faith that will move them forward. Should obstacles show up in a couple's marriage, they will need faith to carry them through to the other side. Faith is to trust God. Faith is to have confidence in God. And faith is to obey God. Abraham understood Hebrews 11:1, "Now faith is the substance of things hoped for, the evidence of things not seen. Abraham had no proof, just God's word."

Ladies, will the man that you marry, like Abraham, when tested by God, pass the test? Will he obey the voice of God when God tells him to pack up and go to an unknown place and without question, go? When faced with a tough decision, will he, like Abraham, with no proof, trust God, and take God at His word? Will he be a man that will obey God, and in his obedience, receive his blessing from God? Will he be a husband that will obey God's word, so that you can obey him? Will he build your marriage on a foundation of faith, so that should a test come to your marriage, faith will be the thing that will cause your marriage to pass the test?

6

A King Amongst Men

Chapter 6

A King Amongst Men

The word king is defined as a male ruler of an independent state, especially one who inherits the position by right of birth. He's also a male monarch of a major territorial unit, especially one whose position is hereditary and rules for life.

A man who is a king amongst men has been called by God. He is anointed and appointed for such a time as this. It is God, not man, who has placed him in his position. A king amongst men is one who is led by the Holy Spirit, His life is centered around God. And God is the center of his life. He is a representative of Jesus, an ambassador for the kingdom of God. People will know that he has been with Jesus because his speech and actions will give him away.

One of the men who was called by God and appointed king, is King David. We know that David was chosen by God to be king because God looked at David's heart. The Bible says in 1 Samuel 16:6-7, So it was, when they came, that he looked at Eliab and said, surely, the LORDs anointed is before Him. But the LORD said to Samuel, "Do not look at his appearance or at his physical stature, because I refused him. For the LORD does not see as man sees; for man looks at the outward appearance, but the LORD looks at the heart." You see, man will often look at the outward appearance of a person and look for their goodness. But God does not operate that way; He chooses kings by looking at the goodness of their hearts.

35

The Bible says that David's father, Jesse, called his son Abinadab, and made him pass before Samuel. But Samuel said that the LORD had not chosen him. The Bible says that Jesse made seven of his sons pass before Samuel. But Samuel again said that the LORD had not chosen these. The Bible says that in 1 Samuel 16: 11-12, And Samuel said to Jesse, "Are all the young men here?" Then he said, "There remains yet the youngest, and there he is, keeping the sheep."

And Samuel said to Jesse, "Send and bring him. For we will not sit down until he comes here." So, he sent and brought him in. Now he was ruddy, with bright eyes and good looking. And the LORD said, "Arise, anoint him; for this is the one."

David was looked over by his very own father because his outward appearance didn't match what Jesse thought a king should look like. What Jesse could not see was that David was a king amongst his all his brothers. The oil would not flow until it got to David's head. You see, God was the One who was pouring the oil, not man. David had been set apart from the rest of his brothers by God. David's father tried to make all of David's older brothers' king, but God had already set David apart to be a king amongst his brothers.

A king is the anointed representative of the LORD. He has been called by God. God has seen his heart and has set him apart from other men so he can do the work of God. A king amongst men has been chosen by God. God is the One who has poured the oil. He is able to lead God's people with wisdom. He puts God first. He is an honorable man of God; all that he says shall come to pass. A king amongst men holds a position of power. He is well respected amongst his peers. The Bible says in 1 Samuel 18:30 that, "David behaved more wisely than all the servants of Saul, so that his name became highly esteemed." A king amongst men is an influencer. When he walks into a room, he is shown honor and respect.

A king amongst men is a friend of God. He is a man who loves and honors his wife. In the presence of his enemies, his table is set. Because he is a king, he must have a queen. She will prepare his bath water and listen closely to him speak. A king amongst men is loved. And he corrects with love. A king amongst men will practice what he preaches. His good character shows who he really is. He is teachable. He is a visionary and a dreamer. He is a man of integrity. He is loyal and honest. He does not take bribes or practice reckless acts. A king amongst men humbles himself before the LORD God. He owns up to his mistakes and extends a palm branch to anyone that he has offended. He is seated with dignitaries and other blessed men of God. He is a man after God's own heart.

When faced with tough decisions, a king amongst men will inquire of the LORD. He will be a praying man. A king amongst men stands out in a crowd and people are drawn to his spirit. He is a man that when he has been given a chance to take vengeance on his enemy, he speaks the words of David in 1 Samuel 24:12-13, "Let the LORD judge between you and me, and let the LORD avenge me on you. As the proverb of the ancient says, wickedness proceeds from the wicked. But my hand shall not be against you." A king amongst men is a man of faith and is obedient to God. He is surrendered and submitted to God's Sovereign will. A king amongst men is standing, in the very presence of God. He is walking in his kingdom assignment, and he knows his purpose.

A king amongst men walks with God and talks with God. He is called by God to do the work of God's kingdom. He has been appointed and anointed by God. A king is the most important member of his family. He is considered to be the head of his family. He takes care of his family; he is a provider. A king amongst men is faithful to his wife because he is faithful to God. A king amongst men is faithful to God's Word. He is not just a hearer of God's word, but also a doer of it. He shows mercy to the ones who have done him wrong. He can echo Joseph's words and say, "You meant evil against me, but God used it good. So, that God's perfect plan should come to pass." A king amongst men can say that there are times when things come against him that seem evil, but he understands that God can use these situations for his good.

Ladies, will the man that you marry be a king amongst men? Will he be an anointed representative of God? Will God look in his heart and see that it is after Him? Will he be able to lead God's people with godly wisdom? Will he be set apart from other men so that he can do the work of God? Will his good character speak for him? If given a chance to take revenge on his enemies, will he repay evil for evil or evil for good? Will he understand that vengeance is not his, but it's the LORD'S. When faced with a tough decision, will he seek the LORD and pray what David prayed, "Shall I pursue this?" Will he be a dreamer and a visionary, because he knows that Proverbs 29:18 says, "Where there is no vision, the people perish; but he that keeps the law; happy is he." Ladies, will he be a man of integrity, honest and loyal? Will he humble himself before the LORD God? Ladies, will he be a man after God's very own heart? Will he be a praying man and follow God's perfect plan for his life despite the obstacles that may come before him? Will he own up to his mistakes and extend a palm branch to the ones he has offended? Will he show mercy to those who have done him wrong? Can he say to them, "What you meant for evil, God intended it for my good, so that God's perfect plan shall come to pass?" Will he be a king that is faithful to you, because he is faithful to God?

7

Don't Marry the Wrong Man

Chapter 7

Don't Marry the Wrong Man

arriage is a huge decision to make. We have already established in earlier chapters that marriage, according to the Bible, is a Covent with God. Marriage is something that should not be taken lightly. Marriage is not like purchasing a new car and once you get the car home, you call the dealership to tell them that you have changed your mind. Marriage is something that should be prayed about before couples enter it. Couples should always seek godly counsel before they get married. Couples should turn to the Word of God for wisdom and knowledge concerning marriage. Couples should be sure that they are ready for marriage before they enter the covenant of marriage.

The word "wrong" is defined as: not correct or true; incorrect, unjust, dishonest, immoral. It is an unsuitable or undesirable manner or direction, mistaken, illegal, against the law, unlawful, lawless, misdeed, offense, injury, crime.

Wow! There is nothing good about this word. Ladies, to marry the wrong man would mean that you are in an incorrect, dishonest, immoral, unlawful marriage. If you were to marry the wrong man according to the dictionary, you would be committing a crime. But how do you know if you are marrying the wrong man? Well, let's look at some men in the Bible that probably could shed some light on what kind of man not to marry. Ladies, these men that made the list from the Bible would probably be the wrong kinds of men to marry. Not all these men were all bad, but some of their actions and characteristics are very questionable.

40

A Man Like Judas

Judas was one of Jesus' twelve disciples who was a part of Jesus' three-year earthly ministry. He was one of the twelve men that Jesus handpicked to be a disciple as Jesus went about fulfilling His earthy ministry. Judas witnessed the miracles that Jesus did. He was around when Jesus gave sight to the blind. And he was there when Jesus laid hands on the sick and they recovered. And he was the person that was given the job to be in charge of the money box. So, what would make Judas the wrong kind of man to marry?

Well, for one, who can forget the major role that Judas played in helping with Jesus' arrest. Judas was the one who snitched on Jesus for just a few silver coins. Yes, he was in charge of keeping the money box. But the Bible lets us know in John 12:6 that he was a thief and that he often stole from the money box. He was with Jesus for three years. He walked with Jesus. He talked with Jesus. And although he knew Jesus, he didn't have a personal relationship with him. He was in the presence of God, but not present. He appeared to be doing the right thing, but his actions proved that he was doing the wrong things.

Judas witnessed all the miracles that Jesus did. He knew that Jesus was a deliverer and yet he was never delivered. He walked with Jesus, but in the end, he walked away. Judas' actions exposed who he really was. He seemed to be just like the other eleven disciples. From afar, you could not tell the difference. But his actions showed the difference. Judas' lifestyle demonstrated who he really was. Judas appeared to have a good heart when he said in John 12:5, "Why wasn't this perfume sold and the money given to the poor?" It seemed that good words were coming from his mouth and good deeds were flowing from his heart, until we get to John 12:6 that says, "He did not say this because he cared about the poor but because he was a thief; as keeper of the money bag, he used to help himself to what was put in."

You see, Judas was just playing a role. He had everyone fooled except for Jesus. But Jesus knew this the entire time. The Bible says in John 6:70, "Then Jesus replied, 'Have I not chosen you, the Twelve? Yet one of you is a devil.'" Judas could fool the other eleven, but he couldn't with Jesus. Judas wore a disguise. He camouflaged himself well along with the other disciples. He played the part as a follower of Jesus Christ very well. He seemed to fit right in with the others. He was able to mask his real identify, but eventually his true character was exposed through his actions who he really was.

Ladies, will the man that you marry be a man like Judas, who was a false flower of Jesus Christ? Will he, like Judas, know Jesus, yet lack a personal relationship with Him? Will he be in very presence of God but not be present? Will he appear to be doing the right thing, but his actions prove him different? Will he know Jesus to be a deliverer, but never be delivered? Will he walk with Jesus, but then when an opportune time comes, he walks away? Will he, like Judas, be wearing a disguise, camouflaging himself with the other disciples of Jesus? Will he be able to mask his true identify, but then be exposed of his real identify by his actions and characteristics prove who he really is? Will he be able to fool everyone around him with a form of religion but lack righteousness? Will evil words come from his mouth and corrupt deeds flow from his heart? Will his actions and the words that he speaks like Judas prove that evil rules his heart?

A Man Like Jacob

I chose Jacob as an example of the wrong kind of man to marry because even though Jacob was a man of God, and God used him in an extraordinary way, he did some things that would make him somewhat questionable as the kind of man that you may consider

42

marrying. He was the son of Isaac and the grandson of Abraham. Jacob went from being named Jacob until God changed his name to Israel. From Jacob came the twelve tribes of Israel. I'm not questioning Jacob's relationship with God, but his relationships with women. Below is a short summary of Jacob's relationships with women.

Jacob was the son of Isaac and Rebekah He had a twin brother by the name of Esau. Due to some unforeseen circumstances, Jacob had to leave his homeland. He traveled to Haran where he met his Uncle Laban. Jacob settled in Haran, working as a shepherd for his Uncle Laban. Jacob noticed Laban's daughter Rachel and offered to work for seven years for Rachel in exchange for marrying her. Jacob loved Rachel deeply. And after working for his Uncle Laban for seven years, Jacob was ready to marry Rachel.

But Laban deceived Jacob and instead gave Leah, Rachel's older sister, as his wife. Jacob was disappointed; after all, he had worked for his uncle as a shepherd for seven years so that he could someday marry the women of his heart. I can only imagine what Jacob was going through emotionally. Here's Rachel, this beautiful woman whom he loved, but now he's stuck with her sister Leah, a woman that he has no feelings for.

And on top of it all, the Bible says in Genesis 29:17 that, "Leah had eyes that were weak, which means she wasn't very attractive. Rachel was beautiful in form an appearance. So, here you have this beautiful women Rachel that Jacob was so in love with. And now he is given Leah, who wouldn't turn many heads when she walked into the room. Jacob didn't love Leah, and he probably wasn't attracted to her. The situation was not working in Jacob's favor until Laban comes up with a plan. He tells Jacob that he can work another seven for him and then he would give Rachel to Jacob to marry. Jacob agrees to this deal. The Bible says that because Jacob loved Rachel so much, the years didn't seem so long. After seven additional years, Jacob finally marries Rachel.

But there is just one problem. Jacob still has Leah as his wife. Throughout their entire marriage, Leah had to fight for Jacob's love and attention. She was always going to always be second place to her sister Rachel. She was in Jacob's presence, but never in his heart. Jacob was physically around, but mentally somewhere else. Leah had to share her husband with another woman, a woman that her husband loved very much. Jacob's heart was never with Leah because it was always with her sister, Rachel. Leah was married to a man whose heart never let go of another woman.

Jacob had his mind and his heart set on Rachel but inconveniently ended up with her sister, Leah. Jacob couldn't fully commit his heart to Leah because he had already given it to Rachel. Jacob could never fully be the husband that Leah wanted him to be because he wanted to be with someone else. Leah tried to make Jacob love her, but that was a struggle when the man that she loved preferred someone else. You see, Jacob was stuck on Rachel, and he would never fully be able to commit fully to Leah. He had given his heart to someone else. Yes, Jacob had married Leah not because he wanted to but because he was pressured to. He never picked Leah for himself; she was picked for him. Jacob had two wives, but his heart was with only one.

Ladies, will the man that you marry be a man like Jacob? Will his heart never fully be with committed to you because it's with someone else? Will his eyes and his heart be set on another woman, but inconveniently marry you? Will he, like Jacob never give his heart fully to you because he's already given it to someone else? Will he, like Jacob never be the husband that you need him to be because he really wants to be with someone else? Will you, like Leah, struggle in a marriage trying to make the man stay with you when he really prefers someone else. Will he, like Jacob, be stuck in his past relationship, that he can never fully be committed to his present one? Will he be like Jacob, marry you not because he wants to, but because he feels pressured to?

Will he physically be with you, but his mind is always with someone else, in his presence but never in his heart? Like Leah, will you have to share your husband with another woman, being second to the woman that he really loves? Remember, although Jacob married Leah, he really wanted Rachel. Ladies, make sure that the man that you marry really wants you and not his past relationship.

A Man Like Sampson

The Book of Judges records in Chapter 13 that Sampson's mother was barren and had no children. But an Angel of the LORD appeared to her and said to her, "Indeed, you are barren and have borne no children, but you shall conceive and bear a son." The angel then told her to be careful not to drink wine or similar drink, and not to eat anything unclean. For she would conceive and bear a son. That no razor shall come upon his head, for the child shall be a Nazirite to God from the womb. And that he would help deliver Israel out of the hand of the Philistines.

Chapter 13 in the Book of Judges says that the woman bore a son and called his name Sampson, and the child grew. And that the LORD blessed him. And the Spirit of the LORD began to move upon him at Mahaneh-dan between Zorah and Eshtaol. Sampson was a man who had been given supernatural physical strength but displayed moral weakness. Sampson was a judge for twenty years. God had sent word by an angel that Sampson would be set apart to God. Even though Sampson was set apart by God, he kept breaking the rules of the Nazarite. Sampson was an Israelite. He followed ways of a Nazarite life. This included not drinking or cutting his hair.

Sampson made a poor decision in letting his power be taken away by the Philistines, all because he foolishly trusted a woman that he really cared about by the name of Delilah. Delilah was approached by the lords of the Philistines to entice Sampson and find out where his great strength lies, and by what means they could overpower him so that they could bind and afflict him. They offered to give her money in return. Sampson confided in Delilah. He told her that his super strength came from his hair. And that if it was to be cut off, he would lose his strength.

Even though Sampson was flawed, God still used him to accomplish His will. Sampson was strong and faithful, but weak and challenged. Sampson had a gift, but he didn't have the wisdom to go alone with it. He made poor choices. Judges 16:6 says that Delilah said to Sampson, "Please tell me where your great strength lies, and with what you may be bound to afflict you." I'm not sure why Sampson would tell anyone the source of his strength? After Delilah continued to pressure Sampson, he told Delilah the truth.

Judges 16:17 says, "That he told her all his heart, and said to her, no razor has ever come upon my head, for I have been a Nazarite to God from my mother's womb. If I am shaven, then my strength will leave me, and I shall become weak, and be like any other man." Sampson made a foolish mistake. He was a man of faith, but he also was a man of the flesh. This was proven in his poor decision making. He missed opportunities to pray and seek God. Sampson decided not to rely on the strength of God but choose to rely on his own power. Sampson neglected to seek God's wisdom but chose to lean on his own understanding. Sampson played with the gift that God had given him. He came up with riddles that he used, along with his gift, to make bets. He used his gifts to intimidate people, he knew that out of fear, they would not challenge him. He used his gift to play on Delilah's emotions. He made a game out of what God had gifted him with. Sampson forgot that his gift was never given to him for his sole purpose but for God's. God still used Sampson for His will, but in the end, Sampson paid a price for his continual and willful disobedience to God. Sampson was flawed. He continued committing sinful acts, but God still used Sampson for His glory.

Sampson had some issues. For one, he had an anger problem. He killed multitudes of Philistines and burned their crops. Through all this, there was God in his sovereignty and grace. But at the end, Sampson paid a price for his sins. Sins have consequences. Sampson chose to align himself with the wrong woman and in the end lost his life. The Bible says that Sampson tried to shake himself free! But he did not know that the LORD had departed from him. You see, in the lap of the wrong woman, Sampson made a foolish mistake. Sampson thought that his strength was in his hair and forgot that it was in God. He was with a woman he should not have been with in the first place. She betrayed his heart. We see that it was only when the Spirt of God came upon Sampson that he had the supernatural strength. Once Sampson foolishly told where his strength came from, he became just like any other man. His supernatural strength was gone. There are consequences to poor choices, and Sampson experienced this truth firsthand. As long as Sampson had his hair, God was with him. When he lost his hair, God left. Sampson had become a free agent. Sampson said that if his hair left, that he would become weak, and be just like any other man. But the truth was if God left him, he would become weak and be just like any other man. Sampson became dependent on his own self, and independent of God and His wisdom.

Ladies, will the man that you marry believe that his strength comes from his gifts and not from God? Will he be a man of faith but also be a man of his flesh? Will he, like Sampson, make poor choices because he neglected to seek God through prayer? Will he choose to rely on his own power and not the power of God? Will he choose to neglect following God when he's been given a position of power? Will he use the gift that God has given him to intimidate others, knowing that they can't challenge him? Will he understand that his gift was not given to him for his sole purpose, but for God's glory? Will he, like Sampson, walk in continual and willfulness disobedience, not obeying God? Will people see his gifts, but God sees his sins? Will he, like Sampson, have an anger problem? And just like Sampson, will he be flawed walking in continual sin, but in God's sovereignty, be used anyway? And just like Sampson, because of his willful disobedience, will God leave him, and he not even know it?

Ladies, will the man that you marry have a gift from God, but not have the wisdom to go alone with it? Will he be set apart for the work of God, but then in his poor decision making, be set up? Will he, like Sampson, be favored by God but also be flawed? Will he have strength and power but then become powerless in the lap of the wrong person? Will he seek his own glory and not the glory of God? Will he, like Sampson, foolishly make the wrong decision because he did not seek wisdom from God? Will he become so caught up in the gift that he forgets who the gift giver is? Will he have the wisdom to use the gift that God has given him, or will he misuse it?

8

You Will Know Him by His Fruit

Chapter 8

You Will Know Him by His Fruit

L adies, say it with me. "Therefore, by his fruits I will know him."

The Bible says that in Matthew 7:15-18. "Beware of false prophets who come to you in sheep's clothing, but inwardly they are ravenous wolves. You will know them by their fruits. Do men gather gapes from thornbushes or figs from thistles? Even so, every good tree bears good fruit, but a bad tree bears bad fruit. A good tree cannot bear bad fruit, nor can a bad tree bear good fruit. Every tree that does not bear good fruit is cut down and thrown into the fire. Therefore, by their fruits you will know them." It's important to note that Jesus is the one who's speaking here. This statement is referencing how to recognize true followers of Christ and the false prophet.

Jesus doesn't tolerate a tree that bears bad fruit. He said that every tree that bears bad fruit will be cut down and thrown into the fire. Jesus said, "That you will know them by their fruit."

Ladies, there are some men that when you look at them, you assume that they are followers of Jesus Christ. But Jesus told His followers that the fruit in their lives shows what's inside of their hearts. There are some men who pretend to know God. They are active in their church, participating in different ministries within the church as in the church choir. They may even be disguising themselves as clergy in the church. They are giving a different appearance to conceal their true identities. They are altering their outward forms so that you will not recognize them for who they really are. They look like true followers of Jesus Christ. Jesus said there are some that act like they know Him, but their lifestyles show what's in their hearts.

A man cannot bear bad fruit if he is a true follower of Jesus Christ. But he can bear bad fruit if he is not. Jesus says that a tree that does not bear good fruit is useless. Ladies, don't marry a man that is bearing bad fruit. Do not align yourself with a man that even Jesus said would be cut off.

Ladies, don't marry a man who is bearing bad fruit? A man like this will not be fulfilling to your marriage. He will not be able to achieve the intended purpose or desired outcome for your marriage. He will not have the ability or specified skills to achieve an expected outcome. He will be useless, unprofitable, unsuccessful, and the marriage will be in vain without success or purpose. He will be unsuccessful in bringing anything into the marriage because he has been cut off. A man like this will not produce a fruitful harvest, but only thorns and thistles.

Ladies, don't marry a man and assume that he has a real relationship with Jesus Christ. Is he a true follower of Jesus or really a wolf in sheep's clothing? Does he not only know of Jesus but also has a personal relationship with Him? Is he applying the word of God to his life? Is he living holy, in righteousness? Is he producing good fruit or bad fruit? In this Bible scripture, Jesus talks about two kinds of fruit: good fruit and bad fruit.

Ladies is the man that you are going to marry producing good fruit. What does good fruit look like? The Bible defines good fruit in Galatians 5:22-23, But the fruit of the Spirit is love, joy, peace, longsuffering, kindness, goodness, faithfulness, gentleness, self-control. Against such there is no law. Or is he producing bad fruit, the things that are contrary to the fruits of the Holy Spirt, which Galatians 5:20 says is, hate, misery, strife, intolerance, meanness, malign intentions, faithlessness, wrathfulness, and uncontrollable passions? Ladies, therefore, by his fruits you will know who he really is.

Why Is Fruit So Important in A Husband?

The first thing to note is that this fruit can only be given by the Holy Spirit. There is no other way to achieve this fruit. The fruit of the Spirit gives nine attributes of a person living in accordance with Galatians 5:22-23. These fruits are the evidence of the Holy Spirit's presence in the life of a believer. When a person receives Jesus Christ as their LORD and Savior, they then receive the Holy Spirit. Ladies the man that you marry should have the evidence of the Holy Spirit present in his life. We know the Holy Spirit's job is to conform us to the image of Christ. He is working to make us more like Him. There's no way to produce good fruit outside of God. John 15:4 says, "Abide in me, and I in you. As the branch cannot bear fruit by itself, unless it abides in the vine, neither can you, unless you abide in me. For apart from me you can do nothing."

Ladies, the man that you marry should be producing good fruits, which are "The fruits of the Holy Spirit" such as love, joy, peace, forbearance, kindness, goodness, faithfulness, gentleness, and self-control. Good fruit is imperative in a marriage. Good fruit will produce good results in your marriage. Good fruit makes for a healthy marriage. With good fruit, your marriage will then be able to thrive, grow and prosper well. Good fruit will develop the right characteristics in your husband. With good fruit, your marriage will live in accordance with the Holy Spirit. Which will then yield positive results, causing your marriage to have a favorable outcome.

9

Godly Men in The Bible, Ladies, Swipe Right

Chapter 9

Godly Men in The Bible, Ladies, Swipe Right

Ladies, if these next set of men from the Bible were modern day men and you came across them on a dating app, you would definitely want to swipe right. These men's characters spoke for them. They were men who had good integrity. They displayed qualities of being honest, and they had strong moral principles along with moral uprightness. They were men who had an abundance of faith. They were obedient men of God; they complied with God's orders and were submissive to His will. They were men that were after God's very own heart. They were men who exhibited forgiving hearts. They pursued the things of God. They ran the race and finished strong.

They were men with godly wisdom. When they were faced with tough decisions, they sought the LORD and prayed. These men were trusted leaders of God's people. They walked by faith and trusted God. God was with these men. When they were in distress, they prayed to God for strength. They listened to God rather than man. They had a purpose and an assignment from God.

Ladies, let's look at each of these men's profiles to see why they would be the kind of man you should consider marrying. Men that have features or qualities belonging to these men, who are distinguished and identify, fall in this class of men.

A Man Like Joseph

Who was Joseph, and why would he be the kind of man that you should consider marrying? Joseph was the second youngest son of his father, Jacob. Genesis 37:3:4 talks about how Joseph's dad favored him over his other brothers because he had had Joseph at his old age. Joseph's dad made a coat of many colors. But when his other brothers saw the coat, they hated him. One day, Joseph told his brothers that he had a dream and that someday his brothers would bow down to him. After he told his brothers his dream, they hated him too. But Joseph had a second dream. And he told his brothers once again that the dream he had indicated that his brothers would bow down to him. Joseph was already being favored by his father, and now he was coming to his brothers, telling them that they would someday bow down to him. This angered Joseph's brothers so much that they wanted to kill him. The Bible says in Genesis 13:18-20, "Now when they saw him afar off, even before he came near them, they conspired against him to kill him." Then they said to one another, "Look, this dreamer is coming! Come therefore, let us kill him and cast him into some pit; and we shall say, some wild beast devoured him. We shall see what will become of his dreams." The Bible goes on to say that instead, one of his brothers convinced the rest of the brothers to sell him into slavery.

Fast forward, Joseph acquired this great position, he was appointed second in command over Egypt. The Bible says that Pharaoh had a troubling dream that no one could interpret. But a servant who Joseph had helped suggested that he summon Joseph so that he could interpret Pharaoh's dream. Joseph said that Pharaoh's dreams meant that there would be seven years of famine and seven years of plenty in the land.

During the famine, Joseph's brothers came to Egypt looking to buy grain. At the time, Joseph was governor over the land; and he sold to all the people of the land. Joseph's brothers came and bowed down to Joseph. The Bible says Joseph's brothers didn't recognize him, but that Joseph recognized his brothers. The Bible says that Joseph revealed himself to his brothers. Genesis 45;4-8 says that Joseph said to his brothers, "Please come near to me." So, they came near. Then he said, "I am Joseph, your brother, whom you sold into Egypt. But now, do not therefore be grieved or angry with yourselves because you sold me here; for God sent me before you to preserve life. For these two years, the famine has been in the land, and there are still five years in which there will be neither plowing nor harvesting. And God sent me before you to preserve a posterity for you on the earth, and to save your lives by a great deliverance. So now it was not you who sent me here, but God; and He has made me a father to Pharaoh, and lord of all his house, and a ruler throughout all the land of Egypt."

Joseph understood that it wasn't his brothers that sent him to Egypt, but it was the hand of God so that there could be a great deliverance of God's people. Joseph forgave his brothers for what they had done to him. But after their father Jacob died, Joseph's brothers became fearful. They believed that Joseph would take revenge on them. Genesis 50:18 says, "Then his brothers also went and fell down before his face, and they said, 'Behold, we are your servants.'" But Joseph's response to his brothers was amazing. Genesis 50:20 says that Joseph said to them, "Do not be afraid, for am I in the place of God. As for you, you meant evil against me; but God meant it for good, to bring it about as it is this day, to save many people alive."

Joseph could have been angry with his brothers for what they had done to him. He could have said, "Now I got you! Remember what you did to me? Now I'm going to get you back!" But he didn't do that: why? Because Joseph understood that it wasn't his brothers who had sent him to this place, but God. He understood the reason for his brothers' evil ways. It was God's purpose so that many people could be saved. Joseph took himself out of everything that was going on and he looked to God for reasoning. Joseph forgave his brothers for what they had done to him. Joseph didn't hold a grudge against his brothers. He had a forgiving and understanding heart. Joseph didn't try to steal God's glory, he understood that it all belonged to God. Genesis 41:16 says, "So Joseph answered Pharaoh, saying, it is not in me. God shall give Pharaoh an answer of peace." Joseph stayed humbled in himself because he was humbled to God.

Joseph asked his brothers the question in Genesis 50:19, "Am I in the place of God?" Joseph also asked the butler and the baker the question in Genesis 40:8. "Do not interpretations belong to God?" Joseph didn't take the glory for himself, but he acknowledged who it rightly belonged to. He didn't try to repay his brothers evil for evil, but he repaid them with good.

Ladies will the man that you marry be a man like Joseph, should a man do evil against him, will he understand that it has been done for God's good, and echo the same words as Joseph did in Genesis 50:20 that says, "Do not be afraid, for am I in the place of God. As for you, you meant evil against me; but God meant it for good." Will he, like Joseph, understand that it wasn't a personal attack against him, but for the glory of God? Will his character of forgiveness manifest when in the face of his adversary? Will his good character speak for him? Will he, like Joseph, be a man of good morals and integrity?

A Man Like Caleb

Who was Caleb, and why would he be the kind of man that you should consider marrying? Caleb was a faithful man of God. Caleb's story can be found in the Book of Numbers. Numbers 13:1, And the LORD spoke to Moses, saying, "Send men to spy out the

57

land of Canaan, which I am giving to the children of Israel; from each tribe of their fathers', you shall send a man, everyone a leader among them." This land that God was giving to the children of Israel was a land that was flowing with milk and honey. It was the place where God had promised them as an inheritance. A place that God had already blessed for His people. It was a place of abundance, and plenty. A place where the children of Israel had been trying to possess for many years. So here they are, they have reached their place of promise. All these years of wondering in the desert, and now they have finally arrived. Can you imagine what this could have felt like? To finally get to this amazing place of promise. Their dreaming had come to an end, and it was now a reality. But before entering this Promised Land, Moses chose twelve men to go to this Promised Land to spy it out.

They were to spy on the land for forty days and bring back a report of what they saw. So, the twelve men returned after spying the land and Numbers 13:27 -28 says they told him, and said, "We went to the land where you sent us, it truly flows with milk and honey, and this is its fruit. Nevertheless, the people who dwell there in the land are strong; the cities are fortified and very large; moreover, we saw the descendants of Anak there." Once the twelve spies returned, ten of the twelve came back with a bad report. They agreed that this was a place that was flowing with milk and honey, but that there were a group of people there who were very strong. The ten spies let fear get the best of them. God had already told them that this land was theirs; all they had to do was take it. The ten spies came back to the Children of Israel with a bad report. They said that they were not able to go up against these people, because they were stronger than they were. They told the people that up against these people they looked like grasshoppers. The ten spies doubted that they could take possession of the land. They became so focused on the people that they lost sight of God.

Caleb was one of the twelve men who went to spy out the land of

Canaan. Caleb was with these men the entire forty days. He saw the same thing that they had seen. Caleb saw a land that was indeed flowing with milk and honey. It was truly a land of abundance and prosperity. Caleb saw God's promise with his very own eyes. Caleb believed God. He knew that God was with them, and all they had to do was just go in and take the land. The Bible says in Numbers 13:30, Then Caleb quieted the people before Moses, and said, "Let us go up at once and take possession, for we are well able to over-come it." Caleb said to the people that the land that they passed through and spied out was indeed exceedingly good land. Caleb told the people that, if the LORD delights in us, a land which flows with milk and honey. "Only do not rebel against the LORD, nor fear the people of the land, for they are our bread; their protection has departed from them, and the LORD is with us. Do not fear them."

But the children of Israel did not listen to Caleb, because they would rather believe the bad report of the ten spies. The children of Israel doubt caused them to forfeit their chances of entering the Promised Land. But Caleb never doubted God. He believed God and understood Him as being a promise keeper.

Ladies, will the man that you marry be a man like Caleb, a husband that's faithful to God? When at a place of promise, will he, like Caleb, believe God rather than a bad report from man. When at a place of God's blessings, will he declare the same words as Caleb, and say, "Let us go up at once and take possession, for we are well able to over-come it." Will he be a part of the ten spies who doubted, or the two spies who believed? Will he be like those men who became so focused on the problem that they lost sight of God? Or will he be like Caleb, so focused on God that he loses sight of the problem.

10

A Heart to Marry

Chapter 10

A Heart to Marry

The heart has a purpose: It pumps blood around your body, delivering oxygen and nutrients to your cells and removing waste products. The heart is an instrument that serves the entire body. What is powerful to note is that the heart of the man removes the waste products from his body. This means that when the heart is contaminated, the whole body is as well. The Bible says that out of the abundance of the heart, the mouth speaks. You will know what's in the heart of a man whenever he speaks. It is his true character that will be made known whenever he opens his mouth. The Bible says in Luke 6:45, "A good man out of the good treasure of his heart brings forth good; and an evil man out of the evil treasure of his heart brings forth evil. For out of the abundance of the heart, his mouth speaks." It can't be any clearer than that.

Ladies, what is his heart speaking to you, good treasure, or bad treasure? It can't be both. Is his heart filled with waste products, things that need to be removed? Is his heart contaminated, impure or corrupt? An example of a contaminated heart is unhealthy, unresolved relationships. Are there things in his heart that are unwanted, worthless, defective or of no use? Could it be addictions or bad habits taking root in a toxic heart? Could it be lust, anger, hate, or a heart barren of the things of God? Or an unproductive heart, living without its purpose? An infertile heart that will not be able to birth any fruitful things into the marriage. A heart that is impotent, unable to take effective action, helpless or powerless?

61

The Bible says in Proverbs 4:23, "Keep your heart with all diligence, for out of it springs the issues of life." Everything comes from your heart. The heart of the man rules him. It is a place of all operations of human life.

The heart is where God looks at the man. Jeremiah 17:10 says, "I the LORD searches the heart and examines the mind, to reward each person according to their deeds deserve." The heart is where God interacts with man. Ladies, if his heart is not right, then the whole man will not be right.

Luke 6:45 says, "The heart is where our choices are made. It is where our will lies. The heart is where the abundance of the heart speaks for us." We can judge the person's character by what they speak. The heart is where you will be able to recognize the man's good or bad behavior by what he speaks. Whatever the man speaks will expose exactly what is in his heart; it will reveal his true character. If he has a good heart, he will speak good things; if he has a bad heart, he will speak bad things. Good will come from a good heart, and bad will come from a bad heard. There's no way to bring good fruit from a bad tree. His heart has already revealed who he truly is.

How do you know if the man that you are going to marry is right for you? Listen to what he says. His true character, his identify will be exposed. If he has a good heart, good thigs will come from his heart. His good character will speak. If he has a bad heart, bad things will come from his heart, and his bad character will be revealed. The heart of the man speaks exactly what the man is full of. The heart of a man cannot lie. If his heart is filled with righteousness, then it will speak righteousness. If it is filled with wickedness, then it will speak wickedness.

Let him speak; it will not take long for you to determine what's in the heart of that man. You will be able to determine what kind of man he is by the things flowing from his heart, and the words coming out of his mouth.

Luke says in Luke 6:45, "The good person out of the good treasure of his heart produces good, and the evil, for out of the abundance of the heart his mouth speaks."

The word abundance means a very large quality of something. So, whatever the man has in his heart, either good or bad, there will be a very large quality of it.

Ladies, the man that you marry should be bringing forth good treasure from his heart. It's what the man will say and do that will reveal what's inside of his heart. Whatever is in his heart will come out through his mouth. If you want to find out what kind of man he is, listen to what he says. Observe his words and actions. What is in the man heart will eventually be revealed by everything he speaks. He can try to mask who he is, but his heart will eventually uncover his identity.

Ladies, if you want to know him, then look no further than at his heart. The Bible says in Matthew 15:19, "For out of the heart come evil thoughts, murder, adultery, sexual immorality, theft, false testimony, slander." If these things are in a man's heart, they will eventually be manifested. Pay close attention so that you don't marry someone with these issues. Don't marry a man with these issues, and then later decide that you didn't know he was this way until after you said, "I do." That somehow, he changed once you married him. His heart had already spoken. You should have already known what kind of man he was, just by what had come from his mouth. If he has sexual immorality in his heart before you marry him, then this will continue after you marry him. A woman is prompted off emotion but a man from his heart.

Ladies, is the man that you are going to marry a man that should stay single? A man that has no idea of what a husband should or needs to be? A present body, but his heart is somewhere else? Will he have the right heart to want to marry you? Is his heart be positioned and designed for marriage? Has God placed a desire of marriage in his heart? Will out of the abundance of his heart speak marriage? Is his heart filled with an abundance of love, mercy, and grace for you?

Ladies, be aware, because there are some men who have hearts that will never desire marriage; they just simply don't want it. They have hearts that have chosen to be single. These men were never positioned, designed, or made for marriage. They can never treat you like a queen because they were never appointed to be kings. They will play around with your emotions. Never settling down for marriage but setting you up for disappointment. These men will just simply and plainly never marry. Their hearts were never at a place for marriage. Their hearts can't perceive or receive marriage. These are men whose hearts were never conceived for the purpose of marriage. It's important to know if the man that you are going to marry has a desire for marriage. Has God placed this desire of marriage in his heart? If not, he is going to be wasting your time. Wasting years of your life that you will never be able to get back again. Be aware of men that will date with no intensions of ever getting married. They make promises of marriage, but never fulfill those promises. They love you with their lips, but their hearts are far away from you. And far away from ever marrying you.

The Issues of His Heart

Ladies, what are the issues of his heart? The Bible says in Jeremiah 17:9, "The heart is deceitful above all things, and desperately wicked. Who can know it?" It is only by the Holy Spirit that the heart of a man will be able to love and forgive. Flowing from a man's heart are his issues. The very words he speaks and every action that he takes will be from the issues of his heart, good or bad. Every word that he speaks is exactly who he is. Flowing from a good heart are good things. And flowing from a bad heart are bad things. The man that you marry will be every word that he speaks. His words will expose what's in his heart. His heart will prove what kind of man he really is.

The issues of his heart will uncover what's really in it. Matthew 15:18 says, "But those things which proceed out of the mouth come from the heart, and those things defile the person." A good-hearted man will speak good things, and his actions will be in step with God. But an evil-hearted man will speak evil things, and his actions will be in step with the devil. An evil heart will produce evil things. Do not align yourself with such a man as this. You will not have to question or wonder what kind of man he is. You will know exactly who he is by what he says and what he does.

Marriage and Divorce

Ephesians 5:32 talks about how God likens marriage to the relationship between Christ and the church. In Mathew 19:3, The Pharisees tested Jesus with questions about divorce. Some of the Pharisees came to him to test Him. They asked, "Is it lawful for a man to divorce his wife for any reason?"

And He answered and said to them, "Have you not read that He who made them at the beginning made them male and female, and said, for this reason a man shall leave his father and mother and be joined to his wife, and the two shall become one flesh. So then, they are no longer two but one flesh. Therefore, what God has joined together, let no man separate."

A man with a hardened heart could potentially lead him into wanting a divorce. Divorce is a result of the hardness of man's heart. Divorce is something that has never been part of God's plan. Divorce is rooted in a hardened heart. It is because the man's heart has so become hardened that he wants a divorce. His heart contemplates, and then plots separation, which then leads to a divorce, terminating the marriage. The marriage is now over.

A Hardened Heart

Matthew 19:7-8 says, "They said to Him, why then did Moses command to give a certificate of divorce, and to put her away?" He said to them, "Moses, because of the hardness of your hearts, permitted you to divorce your wives, but from the beginning it was not so."

Jesus told the Pharisees that it was because of a hardened heart, was the reason for divorce. But that in the beginning, it was not like that. Because of the hardness of their hearts, Moses gave them a certificate of divorce. Jesus lets them know that was Moses that gave the certificate of divorce, because divorce was not part of God's plan. A hardened heart commits lies and infidelity. Infidelity is rooted in a hardened heart. The heart stops loving the wife because it has become so hardened. It stops communicating with the wife because it has become hardened. It has fallen out of love with its wife because it has become hardened. The heart has become selfish in the marriage because it is hardened. The heart has become loveless and selfish because it is lifeless. The heart has become stubborn, unbending. The heart has difficulty understanding how to love.

The root of divorce is a direct result of a "hardened heart" Jesus is telling these Pharisees that from the beginning divorce was never part of God's plan. But it was because of the hardness of the heart that Moses gave a certificate of divorce. It was Moses, not God that gave the certificate of divorce. When a hardened heart is made up and wants to leave, a certificate of divorce is then issued.

A man's hardened heart will lead him to divorce. You see, Jesus didn't say that the reason that Moses issued a certificate for divorce was because of cheating, or lying, or irreconcilable differences. But the reason Jesus gave was that it was because of the hardness of their hearts. The man wanted to put away his very own wife, not because she had done him wrong, but because his heart had become hardened. It didn't want its wife anymore' it was done. His heart had turned him away from his very own flesh. A hardened heart is one that is not easily turned; not even when it's considering a divorce. A hardened heart can be a loveless, and selfish, causing the man to become less sympathetic toward his wife. A hardened heart can lead to divorce; and dress it up in a thing called "irreconcilable differences." A hardened heart will become so different from its mate that it's no longer made compatible.

Even though you may marry a Christian man, this does not exempt his heart from potentially becoming hardened toward you. Even a faithful Christian man's heart can harden. There are some things that can cause a Christian's heart to harden. For example, an offence such as the wrong words spoken from you in a heated discussion, or continual unrepentant sin in his life. It could be a setback in his life or disappointment to cause his heart to harden. Will the trials in your marriage cause him to rejoice or lose his faith, and his heart become hardened? Will he recognize the effects that a hardened heart has on his marriage and pray that God would change it? Should his heart become hardened, instead of asking for a certificate of divorce, he prays, Psalms 139:23-24 "Search me O God, and know my heart, see if there is any offensive way in me, and lead me in the way of everlasting."

Ladies, will the man that you marry be like the Pharisees, who asked Jesus the question about divorce? Will he seek to know if divorce will be an option for his marriage? Or will he understand that divorce is out of the question? Will he want to put you away because his heart has become hardened in the marriage? Will he seek a certificate of divorce or seek God for remorse and pray

Psalms 139:23-24, "Search me O God, and know my heart, see if there is any offensive way in me, and lead me in the way of everlasting." And his marriage can then be restored.

11

Will He Lead You Like Moses?

Chapter 11

Will He Lead You Like Moses?

T he word leader means: A person who leads or commands a group, organization, or country. A leader is someone who sees how things can be improved and will move people in the direction of a great vision. They are thought to be chiefs, commanders. Being a leader can be a tough and sometimes exhausting job. Moses was a perfect example of what a true leader looks like. He modeled the word, "leader."

Moses was a great leader who was chosen by God to lead the Israelites out of bondage from under the hand of Pharaoh. God chose Moses to lead the Israelite people from the bondage of the Egyptians to the Promised Land. This would be a place of prosperity, a place that was flowing with milk and honey. Pharaoh was a cruel leader who was oppressing the Hebrew people. God called Moses to be the one who would help save His people. They had been held in bondage by the Egyptians for 400 years. Finally, the children of Israel cried out to the LORD for help. God heard them and sent His servant Moses to lead them to freedom. God chose Moses to carry out His assignment.

God chose Moses as the lawgiver who met Him face-to-face on Mount Sinai, where God gave Moses the very important Ten Commandments on two stone tablets which the Israelites were supposed to obey. After the Israelites were let go from the hand of Pharaoh, Moses had to lead the people across the red sea. He also had to stand in the gap time after time for the Israelites whenever God wanted to destroy them for their disobedience. The Bible says that in the book of Deuteronomy 9:14, "Let Me alone, that I may destroy them and blot out their name from under heaven; and I will make of you a nation mightier and greater than they." Moses interceded for the Israelites, and God relented.

What I love about Moses is, not only was he a great leader, but he was also given the title "The Man of God." Moses was given the title of "The Man of God" in Deuteronomy 33:1, "Now this blessing with which Moses the Man of God blessed the children of Israel before his death." The dictionary defines the phrase "Man of God" as a holy or devout person, saint, or a prophet. A Man of God is called to be a savior to God's people.

A leader of God should model Moses' leadership skills. Moses had an unwavering faithfulness in God. He walked closely with God. Moses was humbled before God. He obeyed the commandments of the LORD. Moses had to carry the burden of all the Israelite people. Being in this leadership position probably made him extremely overwhelmed and exhausted. But the thing that made Moses a good leader was that he spoke with God face-to-face. Moses was in constant communication with God. He spent days up on the mountain speaking with God. God spoke with Moses, then as a good leader, Moses told the people what thus says the LORD. Moses was a leader who was surrendered to the will of God. He put God first in all that he did. Moses understood that to be an effective leader, he first had to be an effective listener. He was obedient and faithful to God.

Ladies will that man that you marry lead you, by always trusting God. Will the thing that makes him a good leader is that he is a man of God, who is holy and devout? Will he understand that to be a good leader, he must be faithful to God and faithful to His Word? Will he be a leader who is moved in the direction of a great vision? Will he understand that to lead you, he must first be led by God. Will he be a leader with an unwavering faithfulness to God as he walks closely with Him? Will he, like Moses, be in constant communication with God, chosen by God to help lead His people?

12

Will He Provide for You Like Boaz?

Chapter 12

Will He Provide for You Like Boaz?

The word provide is defined as: to make available for use, to equip or supply someone with something useful or necessary, to supply sufficient money to insure the maintenance of someone.

Boaz was a good example of what a provider looks like. He was the husband of Ruth.

Before Ruth married Boaz, she was a poor, widowed woman. The Bible says that Boaz was a landowner. He was a man of great wealth. Boaz owned a field. This is where he met Ruth. Ruth asked her mother-in-law if she could go to Boaz's field so that she could glean the heads of grain after Boaz, that she would find favor in his sight. Boaz came to his field one day and he saw Ruth. The Bible says in Ruth 2:5, then Boaz said to his servant who was in charge of the reapers, "Whose young woman is this?" The Bible says that the servant that was in charge of the reapers told Boaz that Ruth was a Moabite woman who had come back with Naomie and that she asked to glean and gather after the reapers among the sheaves. They told Boaz that she had been working from morning until now; and that she had rested a little in the house.

Boaz saw Ruth while she was working in the fields, gleaning. He wanted to know who this woman was. He was interested in her. The Bible says in Ruth 2:8-9, Then Boaz said to Ruth, "You will listen, my daughter, will you not? Do not go to glean in another field, nor go from here, but stay close by my young woman. Let your eyes be on the field which they reap and go after them. Have I not commanded the young men to touch you? And when you are thirsty, go to the vessels and drink from what the young men have drawn." Boaz wanted to provide for Ruth. He provided a field for her to reap in. And when Ruth got thirsty, Boaz provided a vessel of water for her to quench her thirst. Boaz didn't want Ruth to collect any more leftovers, but he wanted her to have the best. All Ruth had to do was just set her eyes on the field, and it was hers. Boaz was already providing for Ruth before he married her. Ruth could not understand why she had found favor in Boaz's sight. Boaz told Ruth that he had heard all that she had done for her mother-in-law. He told her that she had left her father and mother and how she had come to stay with people that she did not know. Boaz said in Ruth 2:12, "The LORD repays your work, and a full reward be given to you by the LORD God of Israel, under whose wings you have come for refuge." Boaz recognized that it was the LORD who was repaying Ruth for her work. God was using Boaz to provide for Ruth by His hand.

Boaz comforted and spoke kindly to Ruth. The Bible says in Ruth 2:14, Now Boaz said to her at mealtime, "Come here, and eat the bread, and dip your piece of bread in the vinegar." So, she sat beside the reapers, and she ate and was satisfied, and kept some back. When Ruth was hungry, Boaz provided her with bread to eat. Ruth 2:15-16 says, "And when she rose up to glean, Boaz commanded his young men, saying, let her glean even among the sheaves, and do not reproach her. Also, let grain from the bundles fall purposely for her; leave it that she may glean and do not rebuke her." Boaz provided bundles of grain for Ruth. The Bible says in Ruth 3:10, Then he said, "Blessed are you of the LORD, my daughter! For you have shown more kindness at the end than the beginning, in that you did not go after young men, whether poor or rich." Boaz said to Ruth that she didn't need to fear. That he would do all for her that she had requested. Boaz told Ruth that all the people in

75

the town knew that she was a virtuous woman. Boaz reassured her that she didn't need to fear. He let her know that he had heard good things about her. Boaz provided Ruth with all that she requested. Ruth stayed virtuous in the sight of Boaz. Ruth 3:14-15. "So, she lay at his feet until morning, and she arose before one could recognize another." Then he said, "Do not let it be known that the woman came to the threshing floor."

Also, he said, "Bring the shawl that is on you and hold it." And when she held it, he measured six ephas of barley, and laid it on her. Then she went into the city. Boaz provided Ruth with six ephas of barley. Ruth told her mother- in-law Naomia that Boaz had given her six ephas of barley. And that he didn't want her to go away empty-handed. Boaz provided for her empty hand by giving her the six ephas of barley.

Ladies, will the man that you marry provide for you like Boaz provided for Ruth? And just like Boaz, will he own his own field so that you can glean from it? Will he, like Boaz, be a man of wealth? And just like Ruth, when you are thirsty, will the man that you marry provide water for you to drink? Will he speak the same words to you that Boaz spoke to Ruth when he said, "He didn't want her to have the leftovers, but that he wanted her to have the best." Will he provide for you like Boaz provided for Ruth in Ruth 2:9 when he said, "Let your eyes be on the field which they reap and go after them." And just like Boaz, will the man that you marry start the provision before you are married, because the way he starts is the way he will finish?

Will the man that you marry pray for you like Boaz prayed for Ruth in Ruth 2:12? "The LORD repays your work, and a full reward be given to you by the LORD God of Israel, under whose wings you have come for refuge." Will he, like Boaz when you are hungry, provide for you food, so much that you will eat and be satisfied? Will he recognize that you are a virtuous woman with high moral standards, living an excellent upright life, and echo the same words as Boaz did in Ruth 3:10. "Blessed are you of the LORD, my daughter! For you have shown more kindness at the end than the beginning, in that you did not go after young men, whether poor or rich." Will he see your goodness and know that the LORD is with you? And just like Boaz valued and respected Ruth, will he do the same for you?

13

Will he Protect You Like Joseph?

Chapter 13

Will he Protect You Like Joseph?

The word protect is defined as: to keep safe from harm or injury, to defend or guard someone from danger or loss, to shield a person from danger, pain, violence, prosecution, or discomfort.

Joseph was the husband of Mary. The Bible says in Matthew 1:18-21, "Now the birth of Jesus Christ was as follows: After His mother Mary was betrothed to Joseph, before they came together, she was found with child of the Holy Spirit. Then Joseph, her husband, being a just man, and not wanting to make her a public example, was minded putting her away secretly."

But while he thought about these things, behold, an Angel of the LORD appeared to him in a dream, saying, "Joseph, son of David, do not be afraid to take to you Mary as your wife, for that which is conceived in her is of the Holy Spirit. And she will bring forth a Son, and you shall call His name Jesus, for He will save His people from their sins."

Joseph didn't want to disgrace Mary. In those days, Joseph could have had Mary stoned to death for this pregnancy, which was the penalty under the law. But Joseph was a righteous man, and this was proven by him not wanting to put Mary to shame. Joseph loved Mary. The Bible says that he thought about these things. And while he was thinking about it, an Angel of the LORD appeared to him in a dream, saying "Joseph, son of David, do not be afraid to take Mary as your wife, of that which is conceived in her is of the Holy

Spirit." Joseph didn't make a rash decision. He didn't cut Mary off or have her stoned to death. Joseph was a man of God; that's why he could hear from God and receive confirmation concerning what he should do. Joseph listened to God. Joseph didn't go out and tell everyone what was going on between him and Mary. He wanted to protect her reputation. He wanted to protect her from any harm. Joseph wanted to protect Mary from being shamed and persecuted by the town's people. Joseph loved Mary, so for that reason, he wanted to protect her from any harm or danger.

The Bible says that Joseph was a just man. Joseph was living in a right relationship with God. He was a man that had high moral standards. Joseph's actions were justified under the circumstances. Joseph was justified by his response to Mary's pregnancy. Just as God is just and loving, so was Joseph toward Mary. He showed compassion to Mary. Here you have this man, Joseph who is set to marry this young woman. And just as he is about to marry her, he finds out that she is pregnant, and the child is not his. Can you imagine, Mary had been promised to Joseph for marriage, when she comes up pregnant, but he's not the father. But Joseph wanted to protect Mary from being shamed. He didn't want to disgrace her. He thought about putting her away secretly. Joseph didn't want to cause Mary any pain.

Ladies, will the man that you marry be like Joseph as a protector, keeping you safe from harm or injury? Will he be a just man of God, being in right relationship with Him, so that he can hear what God is saying about you? Will he, like Joseph, before he makes a rash decision, think on the matter, and receive confirmation from God? And just like Joseph, will he protect you in the marriage by making the right decisions? Will he keep you comfortable should there be an uncomfortable, difficult situation? Will he be your defender, should there be an attack made against you?

14

Will He Love You like Jesus?

Chapter 14

Will He Love You like Jesus?

The word love is defined as an intense feeling of affection. The Bible defines love as 1 Corinthians 4:8 that says, "Love is patient, love is kind. It does not envy, it does not boast, it is not proud. It is not rude, it is not self-seeking, it is not easily angered, it keeps no record of wrongs. Love does not delight in evil but rejoices with the truth. It always protects, always trusts, always hopes, always preserves. Love never fails." The love of Jesus is never failing. His faithful love is priceless. 1 John 4:8 says, "Anyone who does not love does not know God, because God is love." Ladies, if a man knows God, he will know love, and if he knows love, then he will know how to love you.

Jesus Christ is the perfect example of love. Jesus showed love in Luke 23:34 when He said, "Father, forgive them, for they know not what they do." Even as He hung on the cross dying, he showed love by forgiving them.

I understand that the man that you marry cannot be perfect, as Jesus is perfect. But he should have a heart who wants to model Jesus Christ. The Bible says that we are made in the very image and likeness of God. To be made in the image of God is to allow the very nature of God to be manifested in our lives. The man that you marry should have the appearance of Jesus Christ manifested in his life. His ways and actions should be a resemblance of Jesus. His lifestyle should mirror the lifestyle of Jesus'. To be made in the image of God is to be an Ephesians 4:24 husband. And put on a new self, created after the likeness of God in true righteousness and holiness.

Ladies, will the man that you marry have put on a new self, created after the likeness of God in true righteousness and holiness? Will his lifestyle mirror in the very image of Jesus'? Will he understand that to be in the image of Jesus is to be more like Him? Ladies, will he understand, that for him to fully love you like Jesus, he must fully know Jesus. Will he be a man, like Jesus, who is perfect, love you in your imperfections?

Will he love you like Jesus in 1 John 13:34-35? "I give you a new commandment: Love each other. Just as I have loved you, so you also must love each other. This is how everyone will know that you are my disciples when you love each other." Ladies, will the man that you marry be known and recognized as a disciple, a personal follower of Jesus by everyone just by the way he loves you? Will he love you like Jesus in Jeremiah 31:3, The LORD has appeared of old to me, saying, "Yes, I have loved you with an everlasting love; Therefore, with loving kindness, I have loved you." Will he love you like Jesus, with an everlasting love, and will with loving kindness, love you?

Will he love you like Jesus in 1 John 3:18 that says, "Dear children, let us not love with words or speech but with actions and in truth." Will he love you not just in words and speech, but also in actions and truth? Will he have an unfailing love for you, just as Jesus does? Will he be grown in his knowledge and relationship of Jesus Christ? Because to know Jesus, is to love you.

Will he keep his marriage covenant with you and show an everlasting loyalty to you with all his heart? Will he understand that love is from God, and the only way to give love is to know God. Will he show his love by being faithful to you? Will he love you deeper and stronger every day? Will he have the power to grasp love's width and length, height and depth, a deep intensity of love for you. Will he love you like Jesus in Psalm 86:15 "But you, my LORD are a God of compassion and mercy; you are very patient and full of faithful love." Will the man that you marry be a man of compassion, mercy, and of faithful love toward you?

Will he love you like Jesus in Isaiah 54;10 "The mountains may shift, and the hills may be shaken, but my faithful love won't shift from you, and my covenant of peace won't be shaken; says the LORD, the one who pities you." Will his faithful love for you never shift? Will there be a covenant of peace that never shakes in your marriage? Will he love you like Jesus in Lamentations 3:22-23? "Certainly the faithful love of the LORD hasn't ended: certainly, God's compassion isn't through! They are renewed every morning. Great is your faithfulness." Ladies, will the man that you marry have faithful love for you that never ends? Will his compassion for you be without change, and his love for you be renewed every morning?

Ladies, the man that you marry should love you as Christ loves the church. You are his bride, his helpmeet. You have come to put an end to his singleness. You are his blessing. You are his Queen. You have been handmade by the hand of God. You are from God, for him. You have come to add stability to him. You are there to help him, spiritually, emotionally, mentally, and physically. You have now completed him. You are the manifestation to his answered prayer. With Jesus' love in your husband's heart, all his actions toward you will be love.

About the Author

Stephanie Ross is a Preacher, Speaker, Author, Women's Empowerment Coach, Relationship Advisor, and Creative Business Strategist. She is the founder of The Women's Empowerment Group LLC, where she works to help empower women by pushing them into their God ordained purposes.

She is passionate in helping to build healthier and stronger relationships between couples, by bringing them into alignment with the love of Jesus Christ. She works to help bring couples into a divine coveted relationship with God, so that their relationships can be strengthened in love. Her goal is to help bring couples closer by providing the guidance that is needed to make their relationships stronger.

Thank you for your support by purchasing this book. My hope is that this book will give single women the support and guidance that is needed to help bring them into alignment with the man that God has predestined them to be with, so that their marriage will be used to change the world.

Thank you and God bless!

Made in the USA
Middletown, DE
08 March 2022

62295858R00050